Garfield

Rebel with-out a Clue!

The alleys are his turf, the streets are his life and the garbage cans are his restaurants. This leather clad cool cat is a legend in his own lunchtime … He plays a mean guitar, drives a cool car and eats junk food! *He's a Rebel without a clue …*

© 1987 United Feature Syndicate, Inc.

JIM DAVIS 1-30

This edition first published by
Ravette Books Limited 1989

Printed and bound for Ravette Books Limited,
3 Glenside Estate, Star Road,
Partridge Green, Horsham,
West Sussex RH13 8RA
by Bath Press, Avon

ISBN 1 85304 202 1

GARFIELD

CHAMPIONSHIP WRESTLERS AND I HAVE ONE TRAINING RITUAL IN COMMON. POWER-EATING

SLURP

© 1987 United Feature Syndicate, Inc.

SCREEE

SLAM!

SCREEE

ODIE?

ODIE?

JIM DAVIS 12-13

SLURP

GARFIELD®

I WONDER WHAT THAT IS?

UP AND AT 'EM, BOYS! IT'S A BRIGHT NEW DAY!

LET'S PLAN THE DAY, BOYS

HERE WE GO AGAIN

FIRST ITEM OF BUSINESS: THE CHRISTMAS TREE. LET'S LEAVE IT UP A WHILE LONGER

© 1987 United Feature Syndicate, Inc.

TRANSLATION! "LET'S LEAVE THE TREE THERE TILL THE NEEDLES FALL OFF AND MOM TAKES IT OUT FOR ME IN JULY"

NEXT ITEM: LET'S GO TO A MUSEUM OR SOMETHING INTELLECTUALLY STIMULATING RIGHT AFTER LUNCH

TRANSLATION: "LET'S EAT TOO MUCH AND FALL ASLEEP ON THE COUCH WATCHING TELEVISION"

JIM DAVIS 12/27

Z Z

I ADMIRE A MAN OF DECISION

JIM DAVIS 1-10

GARFIELD

HEY, KID, ISN'T THAT HALLEY'S COMET?

1988 United Feature Syndicate, Inc.

1-17

RUN FOR YOUR LIFE! IT'S A RABID MUSKRAT!

I LIKE THE PART WHERE HE MADE YOU FETCH IT ON ALL FOURS

OH, SHUT UP

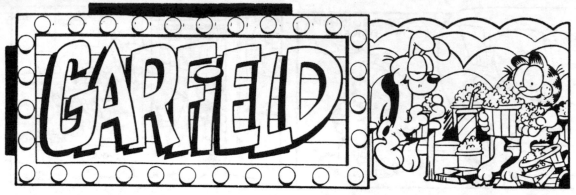

GARFIELD

CRASH!

HEY, GARFIELD, GUESS WHAT?!

© 1988 United Feature Syndicate, Inc.

WE ARE GOING TO ROLLER-SKATE OUR WAY TO HEALTH

JIM DAVIS 3-27

NOW, LET'S GET OUT THERE AND DO IT!

ONE SIDE! HERE COMES YOUR OWNER, THE "ROLLER SKATE KING!"

AYIEEEEE!

HONK!

CRASH!

DOINK   DOINK

THERE GOES MY OWNER, THE "ROLLER SKATE HOOD ORNAMENT"

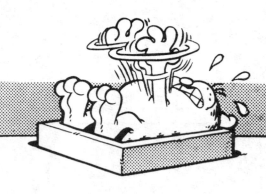

WELL, WHO HAD THE KEYS LAST, DEPUTY?

UH, JON, YOU KNOW HOW CURIOUS CATS ARE, DON'T YOU?

WELL, I SORTA FOUND YOUR CAR KEYS ON THE CHEST AND ODIE. AND I...UH, WELL...

WHAT ARE YOU TRYING TO TELL ME, GARFIELD?

VRMM

© 1988 United Feature Syndicate, Inc.

NEVER MIND

TELL ME, JON, IS IT BAD WHEN THE HEADLIGHTS ARE STARING AT ONE ANOTHER?

JIM DAVIS 6-12

THIS PAINTING OF YOU IS LACKING SOMETHING, GARFIELD

YEAH, A RESEMBLANCE

GARFIELD, ARE YOU LYING ON MY SANDWICH?

YOU MIGHT SAY THAT

9-11

HEY, MISTER, MAY WE BURY YOUR CAT IN THE SAND?

SURE, GO AHEAD

JIM DAVIS

THANKS, MISTER

YOU'RE IN TROUBLE

HAVE FUN, KIDS

© 1988 United Feature Syndicate, Inc.

I MUST ADMIT THIS IS KIND OF RELAXING

THIS SAND FEELS SO COOL...

OKAY, SUSIE, YOU STAY HERE. I'LL GO GET THE ANTS

LIFE-GUARD

DRESSING PROPERLY IS AN ART, GARFIELD

RULE NUMBER ONE, A TIE IS THE EXTENSION OF ONE'S PERSONALITY

RULE NUMBER TWO, NEVER TUCK YOUR SHIRT INTO YOUR UNDERWEAR

HAVE YOU NOTICED HOW ODIE IS ALWAYS SMILING, GARFIELD?

HIS PARENTS WERE HYENAS

WHY DON'T YOU EVER SMILE?

I HAVE MY REASONS

IF HE THOUGHT HE WERE PLEASING ME, HE'D STOP TRYING

JIM DAVIS 9-21

JIM DAVIS 9-22

MAYBE GARFIELD WON'T EAT **THIS** FERN

© 1988 United Feature Syndicate, Inc.

DO YOU KNOW WHAT THIS IS?

I SURE DO

IT'S THE TRIUMPH OF HOPE OVER EXPERIENCE

STAY TUNED

JIM DAVIS 9-24

COMING UP NEXT IS SOME MINDLESS DRIVEL GUARANTEED TO INSULT YOUR INTELLECT

© 1988 United Feature Syndicate, Inc.

JON! YOUR SHOW'S ON!

GARFIELD

MY CRYSTAL BALL TELLS ME I'M GOING TO HAVE FISH FOR LUNCH

OH NO!

GARFIELD! YOU'VE GOTTA HELP ME!

10-2   © 1988 United Feature Syndicate, Inc

I'M LATE FOR MY DATE! WHICH SOCKS SHOULD I WEAR?

JIM DAV'S

MY SHIRT! DOES IT GO WITH MY SOCKS?!

TIES! I HAVE TOO MANY TIES!

THERE ARE TOO MANY DECISIONS TO MAKE!

YEAH, DECISIONS LIKE, SHOULD I ENJOY THIS, OR, SHOULD I TELL HIM HIS DATE IS TOMORROW NIGHT?

GARFIELD

WANNA LOOK THINNER? HANG AROUND WITH PEOPLE FATTER THAN YOU

THE CAT SENSES THE APPROACH OF DANGER

RRRRR

THE DOG APPROACHES, BENT ON WREAKING HAVOC ON THE CAT

AR! AR! AR! AR! AR! AR!

THE DOG THREATENS TO DISMEMBER THE CAT

THE CAT BARES A PERFUNCTORY CLAW

YIP!

THE DOG FLEES, FEARING FOR HIS LIFE

ANOTHER SEARING EPISODE IN THE LIFE AND DEATH STRUGGLES OF HOUSE PETS

JIM DAVIS

10-16

A selection of Garfield books published by Ravette

Garfield Landscapes

Garfield The All-Round Sports Star	£2.95
Garfield The Irresistible	£2.95
Garfield On Vacation	£2.95
Garfield Weighs In	£2.95
Garfield I Hate Monday	£2.95
Garfield Special Delivery	£2.95
Garfield Another Serve	£2.95
Garfield Wraps It Up	£2.95
Garfield This Is Your Life	£2.95
Garfield Sheer Genius	£2.95
Garfield The Incurable Romantic	£2.95
Garfield Goes Wild	£2.95

Garfield Pocket-books

No. 1 Garfield The Great Lover	£1.95
No. 2 Garfield Why Do You Hate Mondays?	£1.95
No. 3 Garfield Does Pooky Need You?	£1.95
No. 4 Garfield Admit It, Odie's OK!	£1.95
No. 5 Garfield Two's Company	£1.95
No. 6 Garfield What's Cooking?	£1.95
No. 7 Garfield Who's Talking?	£1.95
No. 8 Garfield Strikes Again	£1.95
No. 9 Garfield Here's Looking At You	£1.95
No. 10 Garfield We Love You Too	£1.95
No. 11 Garfield Here We Go Again	£1.95
No. 12 Garfield Life and Lasagne	£1.95
No. 13 Garfield In The Pink	£1.95
No. 14 Garfield Just Good Friends	£1.95
No. 15 Garfield Plays It Again	£1.95
No. 16 Garfield Flying High	£1.95
No. 17 Garfield On Top Of The World	£1.95
No. 18 Garfield Happy Landings	£1.95

Garfield TV Specials

Here Comes Garfield	£2.95
Garfield On The Town	£2.95

Garfield In The Rough	£2.95
Garfield In Disguise	£2.95
Garfield In Paradise	£2.95
Garfield Goes To Hollywood	£2.95
A Garfield Christmas	£2.95
Garfield's Thanksgiving	£2.95
The Second Garfield Treasury	£5.95
The Third Garfield Treasury	£5.95
The Fourth Garfield Treasury	£5.95
Garfield A Weekend Away	£4.95
Garfield How to Party	£3.95

All these books are available at your local bookshop or newsagent, or can be ordered direct from the publisher. Just tick the titles you require and fill in the form below. Prices and availability subject to change without notice.

Ravette Books Limited, 3 Glenside Estate, Star Road, Partridge Green, Horsham, West Sussex RH13 8RA

Please send a cheque or postal order and allow the following for postage and packing. UK: Pocket books and TV Specials – 45p for one book plus 20p for the second book and 15p for each additional book. Landscape Series – 50p for one book plus 30p for each additional book. Other titles – 85p for one book plus 60p for each additional book.

Name ....

Address ....

....